T0025536

MY FIRST
Soccer Game

By Alyssa Satin Capucilli

Photographs by Leyah Jensen

Ready-to-Read

Simon Spotlight

New York   London   Toronto   Sydney   New Delhi

For the Shadowlawn soccer stars!
— A. S. C.

To my dad, Ben, who coached me
to shoot a soccer ball as well as
with a camera!
— L. J.

SIMON SPOTLIGHT
An imprint of Simon & Schuster Children's Publishing Division
1230 Avenue of the Americas, New York, New York 10020
This Simon Spotlight edition June 2016
Text copyright © 2011 by Alyssa Satin Capucilli
Photographs and illustrations copyright © 2011 by Simon & Schuster, Inc.
All rights reserved, including the right of reproduction in whole or in part in any form.
SIMON SPOTLIGHT, READY-TO-READ, and colophon are registered trademarks of Simon & Schuster, Inc.
For information about special discounts for bulk purchases, please contact Simon & Schuster Special Sales at
1-866-506-1949 or business@simonandschuster.com.
Manufactured in the United States of America 0318 LAK
6 8 10 9 7 5
Cataloging-in-Publication Data is available for this title from the Library of Congress.
ISBN 978-1-4814-6186-3 (hc)
ISBN 978-1-4814-6185-6 (pbk)
ISBN 978-1-4814-6188-7 (eBook)

This book was previously published with slightly different text and art.

It is my first soccer game, and I cannot wait to play!

I have my ball, my cleats,
and my soccer shirt, too.

This is going to be
a great day!

At soccer I meet lots of new friends.

Coach Green helps us warm up to get ready!

We march like we are
in a parade.

This is fun!

I like soccer already!

It is game time!

We run, dribble, and pass.

Our feet start and stop the ball.

Teamwork is what soccer is all about.

It does not matter
if you are big or small!

There is a big net that is called a goal.

Can we kick the ball inside?

Ready, set, aim.

Now shoot the ball in!

I did it!

I am so glad I tried!

We shake hands with each other.

We give high fives.

We cheer for the other team, too!

Then all of us share drinks and snacks.

Soccer is awesome!

We want to come back!

Do you want to be a soccer player?

Find a grown-up to help you learn the soccer moves in this book!

Don't forget!

In soccer you don't use your hands!

1

Follow the Leader

Jog or run slowly in a circle with your friends.

2

Lift Your Knee

Now lift one knee at a time. Can you balance on one leg like a flamingo?

3
Stretch Time!

Can you move your knees up and down like a butterfly flutters its wings?

That's a great stretch that will get you warmed up fast!

Hooray!

Now you're ready to play!

Dribble, Pass, and Stop

1 Steady the Ball

Put the ball next to the inside of your foot.

2 Dribble

Move the ball forward, back, or even side to side!

Tap and run.

Tap and run.

That's called dribbling.

3 Pass

Buddy up! Pass the ball back and forth to a teammate as you run. That's called passing.
Be sure to practice with both feet!

4
Stop the Ball

Toes up high, to the sky!
Heel down low, way to go!
That's a great way to make the soccer ball STOP.

Kick the Ball!

1 Steady the Ball

Steady the ball with one foot.
Use the inside of your foot
to aim the ball.

2 Shoot!

Kick the ball right in!

3 Uh-oh!

Did the goalkeeper stop the ball? The goalkeepers are the only players who can use their hands.

1

Working as a Team

Soccer is about making friends and working together as a team.

2

Different Teams

When you play in a soccer game, there are always two teams.

Each team wears a different color shirt.

3 Positions

Every person has a special place and position on the field.

Goalie

Right
Defender

Left
Defender

Try them all!

Right
Forward

Left
Forward

After the Game

Be sure to have a cool drink after you play.

And be sure to
have lots of **FUN!**